POTABLE GOLD

POTABLE GOLD

SOME NOTES ON POETRY AND THIS AGE

Babette Deutsch

Potable Gold: Some Notes on Poetry and This Age, first published by W. W. Norton in 1929.

This edition copyright © 2022 Benjamin Yarmolinsky. All rights reserved. No part of this edition may be reproduced in whole or in part, or stored in a retrieval system, or transmitted in any form or by any means, electronic, mechanical, photocopying, recording, or otherwise, without written permission of the publisher. For information regarding permission, write to: Goodreads Press, 454 West 44th Street, New York, NY 10036, or email info@goodreadspress.com.

FOR
Emma Mueden
*in remembrance of her power to make poetry flourish even in the
uncongenial air of the classroom.*

"[Poetry] transmutes all that it touches, and every form moving within the radiance of its presence is changed by wondrous sympathy to an incarnation of the spirit which it breathes; its secret alchemy turns to potable gold the poisonous waters which flow from death through life."

SHELLEY

CONTENTS

Chapter One: *Why Poetry?* 3
Chapter Two: *The Poet and His Audience* 20
Chapter Three: *Poetry and the Machine* 36
Chapter Four: *Whither Poetry?* 50
Chapter Five: *Certain Poets of Importance* 63

THE material of this book developed from a series of five lectures for *The Reader's Round Table* organized to bring authors and users of books into personal contact. The lectures were given in branches of the New York Public Library under the auspices of The People's Institute in the interests of Adult Education during the winter of 1929.

PHILIP N. YOUTZ, *Editor,*
The People's Institute, New York City

POTABLE GOLD

SOME NOTES ON POETRY AND THIS AGE

CHAPTER ONE
WHY POETRY?

It would probably be hard to find, even among practical people, anyone with a genuine dislike for poetry. It would be easy to find, even among the cultivated, many who are indifferent to it. They regard it as something useless and elegant, and therefore, especially if well bound, appropriate as a gift. They consider it something that, unlike the latest findings of the psychiatrists and the physicists, one can safely afford to neglect. They take it for granted, as something that occurs in magazines, instead of a colophon. Those in whom poetry arouses an excitement more or less passionate are contemptuous of these indifferentists. But they are like them in one respect. They too are apt to take poetry for granted. Here it is, a delight to the ear, a jewel to the eye. What does it matter how it came to be, or what it will become? Perhaps too close a scrutiny will dispel its peculiar charm. But I think that poetry is made of more stubborn stuff than such a notion allows.

Originally, at any rate, poetry was no delicate thing,— was not caviar to the general. It appears to have arisen out of the rhythmic chant of tribesmen working or dancing together. The familiar call of the barge-towers on the Volga, the songs of prisoners breaking stone, of negroes hoeing the cotton fields, suggest the crude beginnings of poetry. The thought-content is of small significance here, and it was not much more important in the incantations of the savage priests, which were another well-spring of poetry. Later, verse came into use as a vehicle of narration. When men relied on their memories for whatever traditions, whatever counsel, were to be handed down to the younger generation, and for whatever stories furnished the entertainment of the rich and powerful, they found it easier to cast their tales and sayings into phrases with a strong rhythmic beat. Lines having a regular rhythm are much more easily remembered than the run-on lines of conversational prose. And if there are rhymes with which to tag off the lines, so much the better. Such a jingle as "It was in fourteen ninety-two Columbus sailed the ocean blue" is a classical example of the mnemonic value of rhyme. Of course the device has its perils. There was the boy who repeated to himself over and over: "Columbus sailed the dark blue sea In the year of fourteen ninety-three."

The complexion of poetry has altered considerably since the days of the ballad-singers and the trouvères. But most of us are still savages and children. Our pulses respond more readily to the drum-beat and the quiver of a plucked string than to the cadences of sophisticated verse. Kipling is more largely read than T. S. Eliot. We like poetry to tell a story. The wide popularity of The Spoon River Anthology and John Brown's Body, to name contemporary instances, the steady audience for the Odyssey, sufficiently testify to that. This is not to disparage Kipling, Masters, Stephen Benét, or Homer. The point is that while we continue to take an uncivilized delight in verse that is merely a throbbing of tom-toms and a jingling of rattles, and in verse which does the work of the drama and the novel, there has grown up an enormous body of poetry that cannot be relegated to either of these classes.

Such poetry is, like all literature, a hybrid thing. It is partly a kind of music — at its most primitive, mere drum-beating, at its best, a very intricate, exquisite and exalting arrangement of sounds and cadences. But since its substance is words, and words carry meaning, it is also a way of conveying, with a clarity impossible to music, a statement of fact or an idea. One might roughly classify poets into two groups: those who rely chiefly upon the melodic value of their medium, and those who are more absorbed in the significance of words, regardless of their musical quality.

There are some who believe, with George Moore, that only the first sort can truly lay claim to the name of poet. "Shakespeare never soiled his songs with thought," says the aging sybarite of Ebury Street, "and therefore they are still alive and fresh." His anthology of "pure poetry," that is, poetry untainted by the intellect, opens with a piece of charming nonsense by John Skelton:

> By Saint Mary, my lady,
> Your mammy and daddy
> Brought forth a goodly baby,
> > My maiden Isabel,
> Reflaring rosabel,
> The fragrant camamel,
> > The ruddy rosary,
> The sovereign rosemary,
> The pretty strawberry,
> > The columbine, the nepte,
> The jeloffer well set,
> The proper violet
> > Envied your colour
> Is like the daisy flower
> After the April shower,

BABETTE DEUTSCH

> Star of the morrow grey,
> The blossom on the spray,
> The freshest flower of May,
> Maidenly demure,
> Of womanhood the lure...

With somewhat more of grammar, but scarcely more intellection, so modern a poet as Robert Graves pays tribute to this fifteenth-century master in his own coin:

> What could be dafter
> Than John Skelton's laughter?
> What sound more tenderly
> Than his pretty poetry?...
> So where to rank old Skelton?
> He was no monstrous Milton,
> Nor wrote no "Paradise Lost,"
> So wondered at by most,
> Phrased so disdainfully,
> Composed so painfully.
> He struck where Milton missed,
> Milling an English grist
> With homely turn and twist.
> He was English through and through,
> Not Greek, nor French, nor Jew,
> Though well their tongues he knew,
> The living and the dead:
> Learned Erasmus said,
> Hic, unum Britannicarum
> Lumen et decus literarum.

But oh, Colin Clout!
How his pen flies about,
Twiddling and turning,
Scorching and burning,
Thrusting and thrumming!
How it hurries with humming,
Leaping and running,
At the tipsy-topsy Tunning
Of Mistress Eleanor Rumming!
How for poor Philip Sparrow
Was murdered at Carow,
How our hearts he does harrow,
Jest and grief mingle
In this jangle-jingle,
For he will not stop
To sweep nor mop,
To prune nor prop,
To cut each phrase up
Like beef when we sup,
Nor sip at each line
As at brandy-wine,
Or port when we dine.
But angrily, wittily,
Tenderly, prettily,
Laughingly, learnedly,
Sadly, madly,
Helter-Skelter John
Rhymes serenely on,
As English poets should.
Old John, you do me good!

A dash of old John would do many English poets good. But a whole volume of such tender, witty, pretty, sad madness, however gracefully it may address us, speaks persistently in the thin tones of a eunuch. Mr. Moore's collection includes some of the most delicately lovely madrigals in the English tongue. It foregoes whatever has in it the salt flavor, the tough fiber of primitive human experience, and so cuts off poetry at its thickest root.

Indeed, there does not seem to be such a thing as "pure poetry." This art can never attain to the high abstraction of music. But, on the other hand, it does not aim at the emotionless precision of practical prose. However melodious it may be, it is never free from the entangling alliances of verbal connotations. However thoughtful, it cannot divorce itself from the sentimental values attaching to the sound and shape of words. In this connection I am reminded of John Crowe Ransome's remarkable Survey of Literature:

> In all the good Greek of Plato
> I lack my roast beef and potato.
>
> A better man was Aristotle,
> Pulling steady on the bottle.
>
> I dip my hat to Chaucer
> Swilling soup from his saucer,
>
> And to Master Shakespeare
> Who wrote big on small beer.
>
> The abstemious Wordsworth
> Subsisted on a curd's-worth,

POTABLE GOLD

But a slick one was Tennyson,
Putting gravy on his venison.

What these men had to eat and drink
Is what we say and what we think.

The flatulence of Milton
Came out of wry Stilton.

Sing a song for Percy Shelley,
Drowned in pale lemon jelly,

And for precious John Keats,
Dripping blood of pickled beets.

Then there was poor Willie Blake,
He foundered on sweet cake.

God have mercy on the sinner
Who must write with no dinner,

No gravy and no grub,
No pewter and no pub,

No belly and no bowels,
Only consonants and vowels.

Whatever else the poet foregoes, he must perforce write with consonants and vowels.

Not seldom impatient of his limitations, he is known to express envy of those who, like the devotees of music and mathematics, are able to express themselves more directly. "Beauty is truth, truth beauty," wrote Keats. But truth can be formulated in symbols as stripped of suggestion as this:

$$T = \frac{\pi \times \sqrt{R}}{2g}$$

or this: If two triangles have two sides of the one equal to two sides of the other, each to each, and have also the angles contained by those sides equal to one another, they shall also have their bases or third sides equal; and the two triangles shall be equal; and their other angles shall be equal, each to each, namely, those to which the equal sides are opposite. It is worth noting that one of the finest sonnets Edna Millay has written is a tribute to the author of these bald lines, which seem, at first blush, to have nothing in common with the old unhappy far-off things of poetry:

> Euclid alone has looked on Beauty bare.
> Let all who prate of Beauty hold their peace,
> And lay them prone upon the earth and cease
> To ponder on themselves, the while they stare
> At nothing, intricately drawn nowhere
> In shapes of shifting lineage; let geese
> Gabble and hiss, but heroes seek release
> From dusty bondage into luminous air.
> O blinding hour, O holy, terrible day,
> When first the shaft into his vision shone
> Of light anatomized! Euclid alone
> Has looked on Beauty bare. Fortunate they
> Who, though once only and then but far away,
> Have heard her massive sandal set on stone.

It is not Beauty bare that poetry reveals to us — it is Beauty variously garmented, perhaps clothed only in those trailing clouds of glory that Wordsworth gives to the forgetful soul, but always clothed. The question that arises is why people are not satisfied with music, unadulterated by any adventitious thought-content, on the one hand, and with prose that tells a story or that presents the findings of science on the other. Why — after men had developed the several arts of music, fiction, and drama, and discovered the eternal verities of mathematics, — why poetry?

The answer is that poetry, by reason of the dual alliance which Mr. Ransome and Miss Millay seem obliquely to regret, has something to give us which we cannot otherwise obtain. It may not be something greater, but it is something different, and has a value inseparable from its unique character. Music and mathematics are intellectual pursuits inasmuch as they present a pattern which the instructed mind delights to follow. Poetry presents a pattern, a variety in unity, that offers like surprises and satisfactions. But the noblest poetry is not merely a nice arrangement of consonants and vowels, of stresses and pauses; it is also stained and roughened by a concern for human experience, by the maculations of philosophy. It remembers, with anger and pain, the loneliness and impotence of the old, the impotence and loneliness of the young, the breath on our necks of that guttler, death, and the humbling nets of circumstance about our feet. It is possible not to share the philosophy of Milton, of Wordsworth, of Whitman, but it is impossible to have strong poetry without the force of some equal conviction beating like a heart in its body.

But if in the particulars just mentioned this art differs from those more abstract, how does it differ from prose? Is it, indeed, necessary, is it even possible to distinguish between these two literary forms? The question has long been a bone of contention among the critics. Coleridge defined prose as "words in good order," poetry as "the best words in the best order." Arthur Symons takes exception to this, reasonably enough, asking why prose should not also be the best words in the best order. He goes on to say that "rhythm alone, and rhythm of a regular and recurrent kind only, distinguishes poetry from prose." Mr. J. E. Spingarn declares bluntly that "there is no real distinction between prose and verse.... It is possible, for convenience' sake, to separate the more regular from the more irregular, and to call one verse and the other prose: to say where one ends and the other begins is impossible." With whom shall we agree?

Not, I think, with Coleridge, for prose, whether it have the bare beauty of a Euclidean proposition or go heavily swathed and richly ornamented by the genius of seventeenth-century masters, is, as much as ever poetry can be, the best words in the best order. But what of rhythm? And what *is* rhythm? The author of the article on versification in the Encyclopedia Britannica observes acutely that "the poet knows the law by instinct... He does not compose consciously in 'tribrachs' and 'iambs'; he would gape in astonishment if asked to define the 'pyrrhichian hypothesis'; his bursts of enthusiasm are not modified by a theory of 'trisyllabic equivalence'." If the poet would be embarrassed by having to explain the meaning of these prickly-sounding words, his public may well be pardoned some confusion on the subject. But if we are to understand the nature of poetry, we must be able to use intelligently the terms which define the poet's art.

It may be easier to understand what rhythm is, if we first realize what its absence implies. A noted lexicographer likens rhythmless speech or writing to "the flow of liquid from a pipe or tap; it runs with smooth monotony from when it is turned on to when it is turned off, provided it is clear stuff; if it is turbid, the smooth flow is queerly and abruptly checked from time to time, and then resumed." He goes on to compare rhythmic speech or writing to the waves of the sea. Rhythm, then, is a measured flow of words or phrases, moving now rapidly, now slowly, like the pulse of the human body, and controlled, like that pulse, by the emotion of the moment. But Arthur Symons was talking about a movement more precise than that of the salt Atlantic or the no less salty stuff of life. "Rhythm," he says, "of a regular and recurrent kind only."

What he means here, I take it, is not rhythm, which may be found in all fine prose, but that inalterable beat which, in verse, is superimposed on the natural rhythm of speech: metre. The word "metre" explains itself; it implies measurement. The difference between rhythm and metre is the difference between the living pulse of the sea and the mathematically exact movement of a pendulum.

Before proceeding further, let it be understood that our concern here is specifically with English verse, the technique of which differs fundamentally from that of classical verse. We are dealing, more particularly, with English verse from the time of Chaucer. Though the year of his death, when he was a man of about sixty, coincided with the commencement of the fifteenth century, he may be considered the father of the moderns. Chaucer traveled, on the king's business, in France and Italy, and being a man of parts and devoted to books, he made a careful study of the French poets of his day and also of Dante's Divine Comedy. He imitated their techniques and was, moreover, extremely inventive, and it is upon his work as a metrist that modern English verse is founded. His most famous invention was the heroic couplet, a form which will serve us as well as any other in an examination of rhythm, metre and cadence.

He employs this pattern in The Canterbury Tales. The poet, who was as deeply in love with nature as Wordsworth after him, though responsive to its less awful aspects, is speaking, when the poem opens, of the turn of the year. When, he says, April with its sweet showers has pierced the drought of March to the root, and bathed every vein in a liquor which engenders power; when Zephyrus with his sweet breath has inspired the tender crops in the wood and on the heath, and the young sun has run its course halfway in the zodiacal sign of the Ram; when small birds, open-eyed by night, make melody, nature so pricking them in their hearts: then do folk long to go on pilgrimages. If one reads in the original the lines of which this is a bare prose version, one catches the blend of the then fashionable French tongue with the East Midland dialect which grew into modern English, and one hears, too, belled with lovely rhymes, that steady beat to which has been given the name of heroic verse:

Whan that Aprille with his shoures sote
The droughte of March hath perced to the rote,
And bathed every veyne in swich licour
Of which vertu engendred is the flour;
Whan Zephirus eek with his swete breeth
Inspired hath in every holt and heath
The tendre croppes, and the yonge sonne
Hath in the Ram his halfe cours yronne,
And smale fowles maken melodye,
That slepen al the night with open ye,
So priketh hem nature in hir corages:
Than longen folk to goon on pilgrimages...

In such verse as this, the metrical pattern is easy to follow. It is impossible, however, to abstract a similar pattern from ordinary speech. And it is the contrast between the rhythm of natural utterance and the exact beat in the metrical line that is the distinguishing feature of English poetry. This is less evident in Chaucer, where the sound so closely follows the sense, than in Shakespeare. Consider the opening lines of the hundred and seventh sonnet:

> Not mine own fears, nor the prophetic soul
> Of the wide world dreaming on things to come,
> Can yet the lease of my true love control.

If we follow the metre exactly, we must wrench the syllables out of their proper accent. But the whole charm of the lines lies in the fact that the metre is merely approximated. It is as though one heard, with the inner ear, the five regular strokes of the iamb beating against the accents in the natural flow of the spoken sentence.

The reason for going back to Chaucer and to Shakespeare, if a reason need be given in any discussion of poetry, even if it be modern poetry, is that we must understand the tradition before we can appreciate the significance of a rebellion against it. And the rebellion initiated a few years ago by those poets who banded together under the name of Imagist has a direct bearing on the question of the difference between verse and prose. The Imagists, following the lead of certain French poets writing in the eighties of the last century, discarded the pattern completely, relying only on rhythm or, as they call it, cadence, as the determining principle of their verse. They were not the first English poets to do this, but they were the first to make a battle-cry of it.

For a definition of cadence we can do no better than go to the late Amy Lowell, the most militant member of that curious little company. Cadence, she tells us, is a "perfect balance of flow and rhythm." And in this balance it is not the line that counts, as in regular verse, but the group of lines, or strophe. Now the word strophe originally applied to the lines recited by the Greek chorus as it made one turn round the altar, and Amy Lowell emphasizes the fact that in free verse the movement is a circle or a series of circles. The circle may be large or small, the movement rapid, slow, or even jerky, depending on what the poet wishes to convey, but "the whole poem must be as rounded and recurring as the circular swing of a balanced pendulum."

The difficulty with such statements as this, as Amy Lowell herself recognized, was that they might well apply to certain passages in prose. "What is prose," she asks, as others have asked before and will ask again, "and what is poetry? Is it merely a matter of typographical arrangement? Must everything which is printed in equal lines, with rhymes at the ends, be called poetry, and everything which is printed in a block be called prose?" And she concludes by declaring that "there is no hard and fast dividing line between prose and poetry," quoting the French poet, Paul Fort, to the effect that "prose and poetry are but one instrument, graduated."

Which brings us back to our starting-point. It would, indeed, be easy enough to prove that as between certain passages of prose and others of free verse, provided both are printed the same way, no distinction is possible. And the proof is all the easier since so many poets have stopped writing about roses and nightingales to describe such things as steel rails, broken factory windows and the death of a hired man. One could cite many examples of prose that reads like free verse, as also of free verse that reads like prose. Indeed, practically everyone writing on this controversial subject engages in the pastime of selecting passages of both and inviting the audience to guess which is which. Consider, for example, the following:

> Foam—and the hour is gathered up like mist,
> and we are amid perilous seas
> in faery lands forlorn:
> Wind—and the noises of the town
> are like the humming of wild bees in old woods,
> and one is under ancient boughs, listening ...

and this:

> The beech-leaves are silver
> For lack of the tree's blood.
> At your kiss my lips
> Become like the autumn beech-leaves.

and again:

> An intense copper calm,
> like a universal yellow lotus
> was more and more unfolding
> its noiseless measureless leaves
> upon the sea.

Two of these passages are prose. One is verse. Yet all have a recognizable cadence, all present an image, all exhibit the cardinal virtue of concentration, and all, in so far as they do these things, follow the principles formulated by the Imagist school of poetry. The one difference between the poem by Mr. Aldington and the excerpt from Fiona Macleod's essay, Still Waters, the one difference between that poem and the sentence from Herman Melville's novel, Moby Dick, is that the poem stands alone, whereas the prose bits are snatched from a context that could not be construed as poetry. "It is not metres," wrote Emerson, long before imagism was dreamed of, "but a metre-making argument that makes a poem — a thought so passionate and alive that, like the spirit of a plant or an animal, it has an architecture of its own, and adorns nature with a new thing." Prose, in fine, has its own work to do in the world, the work of elucidation and of narration, and it cannot rest in a single experience, however rich, or feed upon a single emotion, however intense. At most it can pause for a moment to admire the landscape or the stars, as a man, walking from one point to another, may find his business not so urgent but that he can stop to remark a wayside flower or to study a noble skyline. The moment of seeing the flower, of seeing the buildings heaved up against the heavens, that moment of realization is the moment for poetry. All the rest of the journey, from the setting forth to the arrival, belongs to prose. There is, as we have seen, no hard and fast line to be drawn between the two. Prose sometimes talks poetry without knowing it. But one can approximate a definition of these two forms of literature by saying that the one resembles a man walking toward a definite goal, the other is like a man surrendering himself to contemplation, or to the experience of walking for its own sake. Prose has intention; poetry has intensity.

And there, I think, we have the crux of the matter. Poetry, whether it be written in exact metres or in free cadences, whether its subject be Paradise regained or Chicago, hog-butcher to the world, whether it use, with Wordsworth, the language of common speech, or employ the literary elegance of a John Lyly, poetry is in its essence a passionate apprehension of experience. Like music, upon which it encroaches, like pure mathematics, which fills those who practice it with the same ecstasy that poetry produces, it is directed to no practical end. But since its medium is words, and words are loaded with meaning, it lacks the crystal purity of this art and that science. The poet works by suggestion, by association, by a knotting together of the slenderest threads of thought, by a plunge of the whole fabric into the staining juices of life. Poetry is the intensification of experience. It has no issue in action. And that peculiarity is its justification.

Though we live — perhaps because we live — in what is often called a practical age, a hard, power-loving, machine-minded age, there is a place in it for poetry. Poetry that means realization. Poetry that means life more abundant.

CHAPTER TWO
THE POET AND HIS AUDIENCE

BETWEEN the poet and his audience there is a quarrel of long standing. It is bred of the difference between him and them,— a difference which they may be the first to recognize but are, perhaps, the last to understand. He does not necessarily see more than his contemporaries, but he sees more intensely. And because of the intensity with which he apprehends his world, he becomes, whether he is aware of it or not, its mouthpiece.

Tradition is the poet's bread — bread that he accepts as a matter of course, and that he changes, by a kind of intellectual and spiritual digestion, into living tissue. That which acts upon tradition to alter it in this radical fashion is — since the word "soul" is out of fashion — the poet's personality. It embraces, tacitly but firmly, those notions about the universe and man's place in it that are so much a part of the contemporary consciousness as to be taken for granted: the notions that determine the spirit of the age. And then, by virtue of that uncommon sensitiveness and percipience which turn a cobbler like Hans Sachs or a chemist's apprentice like John Keats into a poet, the ordinary crumbling stuff of experience is transmuted — if we may change the image — to everlasting gold.

Now his companions are not apt to realize that he is serving them in this fashion. There remains always a gap between him and them. For while they live in the same intellectual climate with him, they merely engage in aimless talk about the weather, whereas he is a kind of weather prophet. Not fully appreciating what they experience, the common run of people underestimate the poet's view of it. Generally speaking, it is only after an epoch has come to an end, and those who made it what it was and those who interpreted it to itself are all dead together, that the poet comes into his own.

Such a state of affairs does not incline him to concern himself deeply with the opinion of his own generation. Browning might address his audience thus: "... British Public, ye who like me not (God love you), whom I yet have labored for," in the preface to The Ring and The Book. But even Browning could exclaim impatiently, "I never pretended to offer such literature as should be a substitute for a cigar or a game of dominoes to an idle man." The poet's attitude is very generally that expressed by Keats in a letter to Reynolds, à propos of his first haughty preface to Endymion: "The Public; a thing I cannot help looking upon as an Enemy, and which I cannot address without feelings of Hostility." His business was not with the vulgar, not even, indeed, with the contemporary élite. It was — let's not be afraid of a word, after all — it was with his own soul. "I have not the slightest feeling of humility toward the public," he declared in the same letter, "—or to anything in existence — but the eternal Being, the Principle of Beauty, and the Memory of Great Men."

This contempt for the public is not unusual. In her preface to the second volume of Imagist poetry Amy Lowell, having stated that she is about to explain the laws governing imagism, observes: "A few people may understand, and the rest can merely misunderstand again, a result to which we are accustomed." In her short sharp essay on Poetry and Criticism, Edith Sitwell, citing Samuel Daniel's Defence of Rhyme and comparing this seventeenth century critic's views to those of the present editor of *The London Mercury*, deduces "that criticism has not changed — excepting in becoming more vulgar." And a comparatively early poem of Ezra Pound's sums up the poet's attitude so neatly that I cannot do better than quote it in full:

SALUTATION THE SECOND

You were praised, my books,
    because I had just come from the country;
I was twenty years behind the times,
    so you found an audience ready.
I do not disown you,
    do not you disown your progeny.
Here they stand without quaint devices,
Here they are with nothing archaic about them.
Watch the reporters spit,
Watch the anger of the professors,
Watch how the pretty ladies revile them:

"Is this," they say, "the nonsense
    that we expect of poets?"
"Where is the Picturesque?"
    "Where is the vertigo of emotion?"
"No! His first work was the best."
    "Poor Dear! he has lost his illusions."

> Go, little naked and impudent songs,
> Go with a light foot!
> (Or with two light feet, if it please you!)
> Go and dance shamelessly!
> Go with an impertinent frolic!
>
> Greet the grave and the stodgy,
> Salute them with your thumbs at your noses.
> Here are your bells and confetti.
> Go! rejuvenate things!
> Rejuvenate even "The Spectator."
>
> Go! and make cat calls!
> Dance and make people blush,
> Dance the dance of the phallus
>   and tell anecdotes of Cybele!
> Speak of the indecorous conduct of the Gods!
>   (Tell it to Mr. Strachey)
> Ruffle the skirts of the prudes,
>   speak of their knees and ankles.
> But above all, go to practical people —
>   go! jangle their door-bells!
> Say that you do no work
>   and that you will live forever.

There are two lines of this refreshingly impudent Salutation that fairly sum up the poet's business and at the same time indicate two sources of the perennial quarrel between him and the public. "Go!" cries Pound, "rejuvenate things!" Rejuvenation, a renewal of vision, a fresh savoring of experience, so that Burns

BABETTE DEUTSCH

can look at a common daisy and Robert Frost at a wood-pile as less sensitive men look at the Crown jewels: this is the essence of the poetic approach. To see a World in a Grain of Sand and a Heaven in a Wild Flower, hold Infinity in the palm of your hand and Eternity in an hour. It is the response of the child, to whom the most everyday matters come with a shock of delicious novelty. The adult's wish, never fully realized, to enjoy again the flavors, the odors, the sounds and shapes and colors that made his childhood wonderful, mistakes its object. It would do him no good to taste the same foods, move among the same furniture, explore the same landscape, breathe the same air of those early days. What he needs to recover is not these things, but the virgin acuteness of sensibility, the innocency of the eye. By virtue of retaining this, the poet is what he is, and one might expect the rest of mankind to be grateful to him for lending them his senses. But along with the desire to feel again the prick of first perceptions, goes an immense, a profound indolence. Man is a slothful animal, hating to be disturbed. And what is more disturbing than a new point of view? So we find the general public admiring the great poets of the past, and ignoring, if it does not revile, the living poets. Wordsworth, Coleridge, Shelley, Keats, were despised in their time. And, as Miss Sitwell has eloquently insisted, it is those who rebel against the tradition established by Wordsworth who are considered outrageous offenders against taste in our own day.

Wordsworth, writing in 1798, was himself in rebellion against what he called "the gaudiness and inane phraseology of many modern writers." What he proposed to do, as his famous Preface to the Lyrical Ballads tells us, was "to choose incidents and situations from common life, and to relate or describe them, throughout, as far as was possible in a selection of language really used by men." He aimed to present such situations chiefly as they occur in "humble or rustic life ... because, in that condition, the essential passions of the heart find a better soil in which they can attain their maturity, are less under restraint, and speak a plainer and more emphatic language...." One need not look far to discover the contemporary poets who are in complete agreement with Wordsworth, and who, indeed, carry his theory into practice more energetically than ever he was able to do himself. The early work of John Masefield, the narrative poems of Robert Frost, the lyric simplicities of Vachel Lindsay, practically every line that Carl Sandburg has written — what do these offer but incidents and situations from common life rendered in the words men commonly use? Such poets as these trace their descent directly, if unconsciously, from the author of the Preface to the Lyrical Ballads. Even the Imagists, who are not particularly concerned with humble or rustic life, echo Wordsworth insofar as their first tenet is "to use the language of common speech, but to employ always the *exact* word, not the nearly-exact, nor the merely decorative word," and their third tenet is "to allow absolute freedom in the choice of subject,"— in fine, not to limit themselves to what is generally accepted as the only possible poetic material.

But there is also a considerable group of contemporary poets who, with Miss Sitwell, are eager to return to "an earlier tradition in poetry" than that stemming from the bard of Duddon: "the great tradition leading from the Elizabethans." It is high time, they declare, to leave "the peasant and words suitable to the peasant." There is a richer, more various, more exciting world to be explored than that of the Lake country, with its rural simplicity, its dull calm. As the Elizabethans, stirred by the strange tales and enchanted with the marvelous cargoes brought home by the merchant adventurers, crammed their verses like a ship's hold with gold and spices and curious creatures, so certain of the moderns delight in the exotic, the decorative, even the grotesque. The best example of this kind of writing is to be found in the work of Miss Sitwell herself.

Take the following passage from her Elegy on Dead Fashion:

> Through mulberry trees a candle's thick gold thread,—
> So seems the summer sun to the sad Dead;
> That cackling candle's loud cacophonies
> Will wake not Plato, Aristophanes,
>
> For all their wisdom. There in the deep groves
> They must forget Olympus and their loves,
> Lying beneath the coldest flower we see
> On the young green-blooming strawberry.
>
> The nymphs are dead like the great summer roses.
> Only an Abyssinian wind dozes;
> Cloyed with late honey are his dark wings' sheens
> Yet once on these lone crags nymphs bright as queens
>
> Walked with elegant footsteps through light leaves
> Where only elegiac air now grieves,—
> For the light leaves are sere and whisper dead
> Echoes of elegances lost and fled.

Certainly there is nothing here of the peasant or words suitable to the peasant. This is neither the description of a common experience nor yet the language of common men. To speak of the sunlight in terms of a "cackling candle's loud cacophonies" is to go back to the "gaudy...phraseology" of pre-Wordsworthian days, when the bee was "Nature's prime confectioner," and a lady's lashes "the fringéd Vallance of [her] eyes." But if Miss Sitwell and her companions are returning to an older tradition, they carry with them the prejudices and penchants of this twentieth century, and their poetry is deeply affected thereby. The Elizabethans may have employed a euphuistic elaboration of metaphor, a thickly allusive imagery; they may even have called the sun a candle, but they would never have spoken of it as "cackling." It is in the use of such an unlikely epithet that we recognize Miss Sitwell as of this century. For words are the flesh and blood of poetry, as rhythm is its motion, and so it is chiefly in the use of words that we are struck by innovations.

In ordinary speech, in prose, in scientific statements, we use words as symbols of things and ideas. In poetry, too, we use them that way. But in literary prose and all poetry we are aware of the thick fringes and fine filaments of meaning that cling to the bare symbol and entangle it with a dozen other meanings, until a single monosyllable can summon up associations as many and as rich in emotional content as can an old photograph, a familiar odor, or a phrase of music. Before a word takes on this ambiguous and enriching character, it is relatively useless to the poet. That is why we have hundreds of fine lyrics about ships, men having gone down to the sea in ships for thousands of years, while we have perhaps two or three acceptable poems about airplanes. When people talk about "poetic diction" they mean words that have been sailing about the seas of literature so long that associations cling to them like barnacles. And indeed, it is when we meet the same old barnacles, as it were, every time, that a word ceases to be truly poetic and becomes a cliché. It loses its emotional values as surely as does a picture that one sees every day and so fails to see at all, or an aria that one hears so frequently that one's ears are deadened to its charm. Words and phrases that have been made over-familiar by constant repetition become the fit material for satiric verse only. Thus we find E. E. Cummings proclaiming:

> ... i would suggest that certain ideas, gestures rhymes, like Gillette Razor Blades having been used and reused to the mystical moment of dullness emphatically are Not To Be Resharpened. (Case in point
>
> if we are to believe these gently O sweetly melancholy trillers amid the thrillers these crepuscular violinists among my and your skyscrapers — Helen & Cleopatra were Just
>   Too Lovely,
> The Snail's On The Thorn enter Morn and God's
> In His andsoforth ...)

The associations called up by the meaning of words are, however, only one of the poet's several concerns. He is also attentive to the suggestions carried purely by sound. That is why he is inclined to take seriously the Frenchwoman who, when asked what she considered the most beautiful words in the English language, made the famous reply of "cellar door." Dissociated from its significance, "cellar door" forms three cool clear liquid syllables such as might lend melody to any line of poetry. The work of Gertrude Stein is the obvious example of poetry built on this principle. But as one examines these verbal patterns, a doubt blocks the doorway of the would-be hospitable mind. Generally speaking, as poetry approaches pure music and, by the same token, pure nonsense, it becomes oddly reduced in stature and "uglified," as the Mock-Turtle would say, in feature. Since words, unlike the material employed by other artists, have certain unescapable connotations, they must fail to respond as gratefully to abstract treatment as colors do, or sounds.

The values attaching to what Robert Graves happily terms the "texture" of poetry are, nevertheless, not to be neglected. They can be studied with rewarding results in the work of H. D. and the late Elinor Wylie. Few lyricists of this generation have been so deeply absorbed as was Mrs. Wylie in the chiseling of a phrase, the manipulation of a rhyme, the poising of light and heavy syllables. Words, their grain and color, their shape and weight, the careful balance of vocables, the nice consideration of consonants, these were her particular concern. She cherished them as she cherished other man-made things: rich stuffs, fine china, gardens, jewels; and she seemed to love her nouns and adjectives for the same reason that centered her attention upon those ornaments and amenities — for the decorative element in them and for whatever reminders they could offer of a sumptuous and gracious life. Hence the smooth immaculateness, the high polish, the orbed and pointed character of her verse. Those noble sonnets which were her final bequest and which are as fine as anything in the language since Shakespeare, gain their magnificence from the fact that she could match intense emotion and intense thought with a perfect control of her medium. Here certainly the substance was at one with the shadow, the body with the winged ghost.

It is no new thing for poets to use words for their allusiveness, and certainly nothing new for them to consider the melodic value of words. What is new is the emphasis that many contemporaries put on suggestion and music. Herein, as Mr. Edmund Wilson has recently pointed out, they are taking their cue from France.

BABETTE DEUTSCH

It is not possible here to trace the history of French poetry, which differs considerably from English. Suffice it to say that toward the close of the nineteenth century there arose in France the so-called Symbolist school of poets, whose aim it was to convey fleeting sensations and emotions by a series of metaphors that called up complicated associations in the poet's mind and in the minds of such readers as were attuned to his, all phrased in a melody that was itself suggestive. The French Symbolists were much influenced by the work and theory of the American poet, Edgar Allen Poe, who relied strongly on the musical quality of verse.

In the performance of T. S. Eliot, and of the numerous younger men who derive from him, as in the esoteric imagery of Edith Sitwell, one finds the principles of the Symbolists nicely exemplified. The difficulty in comprehending much contemporary work is just because the poets are using words and images that are packed with significance for themselves, careless whether these have meaning for a possible audience. Miss Sitwell's verse particularly abounds in words that startle and waylay. It proffers "fruits with a tuneful smell," summer fruits that "giggle insipidly," dew that "whines and cowers," and more involved, more intricate curiosities. She is using here what she calls "a new scale of sense values." More precisely, she is employing adjectives and verbs appropriate to the findings of one of the five senses in order to convey adequately, or at least to her own satisfaction, that which another sense discerns.

In the course of her essay on Poetry and Criticism she is at pains to elucidate a lyric that is full of like difficulties for the unaccustomed reader. And in conclusion she notes that what she is doing in her poetry is after all not very different from what the contemporary painters and musicians are doing in their respective fields. The uninstructed eye looking at a modern painting sees nothing but a confusion of line and color. The uninitiated ear listening to a piece of modern music hears nothing but an incoherent blare of sound. The average reader, coming to the poetry of Edith Sitwell, or to that of Hart Crane or Allen Tate, or to that of their master, T. S. Eliot, or that of his master, Jules Laforgue, is left bewildered. He has to learn their peculiar idiom, an idiom that is in each case distinctly personal, but that in all cases alike seems to be governed by a kind of sensorial transposition. These poets are doing what the artist does when he uses paint to create a form as abstract as that of music. They are doing what the musician does when he uses sound to convey a picture.

But the fact that they are inclined to trespass on the domain of the other arts is not the sole source of the difficulty they present. In their flight from Wordsworthian simplicity, they incline not merely to verbal elaboration but also to abstruse intellection. If the Imagists had a rather tedious habit of writing prefaces to expound their reasons for preferring cadence to metre, the neo-Elizabethans (a word that must be generously interpreted to comprehend a triple allegiance to Webster, Donne and Laforgue) crowd their poetry with pedantic allusions that require the clumsy help of notes for their elucidation.

Further, experience is for them not so much a steady flow of events as a blinding rain of discrete discomfiting moments. They have been looking intently at a world that, for all their earnest, willing and serious study, they fail to synthesize. Confronted with a universe apparently meaningless, they mirror in their verse its broken, fragmentary, confused character. Hence, a good deal of modern work is angular, shrill, wilfully stretched into grotesque contours, like the painting, like the music, like the furniture, like the window-dressing in the fashionable shops of this our day and generation.

Naturally the public, even the intellectual public, is apt to resent the esoteric idiosyncrasies of these artists. But the difficulties the poet presents to his audience is not the only source of its feeling against him. There is another line in Mr. Pound's poem which gives a clew to the ancient feud between the singer and his less articulate fellows. It is the line in which Pound addresses his own songs thus: "Say that you do no work and that you will live forever."

That poetry is an impractical pursuit is no new charge against it. A hundred years ago, in that spirited essay on the Four Ages of Poetry which called forth his friend Shelley's famous Defence of the art, Peacock was writing: "It [poetry] can never make a philosopher, nor a statesman, nor in any class of life a useful or rational man. It cannot claim the slightest share in any one of the comforts and utilities of life of which we have witnessed so many and so rapid advances.... Poetry was the mental rattle that waked the attention of intellect in the infancy of civil society: but for the maturity of mind to make a serious business of the playthings of its childhood, is as absurd as for a full-grown man to rub his gums with coral, and cry to be charmed to sleep by the jingle of silver bells." And longer ago than that Plato called poetry a pack of lies, and said that should one of the dangerous men who made it come to his Republic, though the citizens "fall down and worship him as a sweet and holy and wonderful being," they "must also inform him that there is no place for such as he is in [the] State,— the law will not allow them. And so," proceeds the serene arbiter, "when we have anointed him with myrrh, and set a garland of wool upon his head, we shall send him away to another city."

Now it is true that while the thing the poet deals with usually exists in the world of fact, it is usually unrecognizable by the time he is finished with it. An event cannot become part of a poem until it has been translated to the poet's mind, where, like any immigrant, it is subject to unfamiliar laws and conditioned by novel circumstances. Thus, the Trojan War must have been an actual occurrence,— a conflict between semi-barbarous peoples of related stock living on the islands and along the shores of the Ægean Sea in time beyond memory. But when it took place, and why, and how it ended, is unknown. All that we are certain of is that the story of Troy that Homer tells us is a tissue of history, folk-lore, fantasy and opinion, all steeped in the colors of what appears to be one mind, to emerge a superb and simple whole. What Homer imagined never happened,— so far Plato is right. He is right, too, in declaring that many of Homer's absorbing and exciting lies are calculated to inspire impious thoughts and to feed and water the passions. Shall we, then, fearing Homer, even when he bears us gifts, anoint him with the myrrh of our admiration, set the garland of our praise upon his head, and send him away?

There is only one answer to this question. We are not likely to be led to impiety by his account of the bad behavior of the gods. Since we do not believe in his gods, it does not matter if we do believe in their wickedness. Our passions may well be nourished by what he tells us of Helen's beauty and Hector's valor and Hecuba's grief. But we are not unready to throw meat to our passions. He has not given us historical truth, but he has given us an imagined world of beautiful women and brave men larger than life and more splendid. They are like the Platonic Ideas: immortal patterns of transcendent reality. We may address them as Keats addressed the figures on the Grecian urn: "When old age shall his generation waste, Thou shall remain ...." When twelve centuries shall have passed over her head, will the same be said of Mr. Strachey's Queen Victoria, about whom we know almost everything, and in whose least foibles, as this historian presents them, we delight?

Shelley seems to have the best of Plato when he declares that "Time, which destroys the beauty and the use of the story of particular facts, stripped of the poetry which should invest them, augments that of poetry, and for ever develops new and wonderful applications of the eternal truth which it contains." And Aristotle observes that "the poet and the historian differ not by writing in verse or in prose. The work of Herodotus might be put into verse, and it would still be a species of history, with metre no less than without it. The true difference is that one relates what has happened, the other what may happen. Poetry, therefore, is a more philosophical and a higher thing than history: for poetry tends to express the universal, history the particular." The truth of poetry, then, would seem to be more durable than the truth of fact, and therefore, in a deep sense, the only solid truth. We disagree with Plato, but if we err, we err with Aristotle, so we need not be unduly disturbed over our position in the matter.

So much for the question of poetry and truth. But there is another side of the problem which we have treated perhaps too flippantly. What is the answer to Plato's contention that poetry feeds the passions and, by the same token, sins against reason? Is it the fact that the writing, and more particularly, the reading of verse offers an escape from the doubts and fears and turmoil of life, and lulls us into a forgetfulness that may well breed larger troubles? This question must be answered like the previous one. Like all art that is worthy of the name, it is a widening and deepening of experience, and so a tonic to the spirit. We are living in an irreligious age, without the support of those notions which for so many centuries sustained men in the face of fate and death. Science offers nothing in which to rest. It remains, then, for the arts, for poetry among the others, to give us those moments unvexed by the need for responsive action that can lift us out of ourselves and into the serene air of contemplation. Like noble music, like great painting, like lovely dancing, poetry is a stimulus to and an enlargement of life rather than a refuge from it. It partakes of the nature of all art, and therefore it nourishes not the passions, but the soul of man.

CHAPTER THREE
POETRY AND THE MACHINE

THE title of this chapter should properly be Poetry and This Age: the word "machine" here is used as a symbol of the process of industrialization that is going on all around us, and industrialization is itself the factor that looms largest in a consideration of modern society. But when I have said this, I am reminded that the world about us did not spring from the front of the twentieth century, as it were, like Minerva full-panoplied from the brow of Jove. We are living in a world that was fathered, intellectually speaking, by the seventeenth century. It was then that such thinkers as Descartes and Newton advanced theories which led to an interest in the here-and-now, as opposed to the hereafter. And the philosophy and science of the seventeenth century, with their emphasis on matter and mechanics, led to the materialistic doctrines of the eighteenth century and to the technological advances of the nineteenth. We are, as we are apt to forget, the heirs of all the ages. If we throw the stress a little differently in repeating this: we are the heirs of *all* the ages,— we realize that we are inheriting, along with the mechanistic view of nature popular with our eighteenth-century forefathers, the romantic reaction against that view which occurred in the nineteenth century. And therewith goes our own peculiar slant on the universe. For, as Professor Whitehead points out, "Whereas you can make a replica of an ancient statue, there is no possible replica of an ancient state of mind." What is important to remember is that the poets of our own time cannot begin absolutely afresh: they must stem from the past, just as an individual does who has his grandfather's nose, his cousin's laugh, his mother's short temper, his father's fondness for tinkering, and his own particular selfhood which embraces all these traits and something more that cannot be duplicated.

And just as the individual is apt to resemble his parents, and when he matures to rebel against them, so the beginning of an epoch is apt to be much like its immediate predecessor and only to formulate its difference later on. We can therefore find a good many characteristics of the nineteenth century in the age in which it is our fortune to be living. Before examining the ways in which we differ from it, let us be clear as to what we have in common with it.

First of all, we share the nineteenth-century interest in science. This interest is so dominant that it is mimicked, if it is not actually shared, by the person generally construed as the man in the street. So that although there may be only half a dozen men, if there are that many, able to discuss Einstein's theories with critical intelligence, there are millions who know Einstein's name as that of a great innovator in a particularly abstruse field. Along with our interest in science goes an interest in the machinery that science has made possible. And along with our attention to both, goes a fear of both. We have seen something of scientific warfare, and we are frequently warned that the next war will be waged so scientifically that there will be nobody left to comment on its marvels when it is all over. We have seen machines which were supposed to give people leisure for a fuller and more responsive life turn the men who tend them into a kind of animated machinery. Now in these healthy interests, if not in these well-founded fears, we stand side by side with a poet who lived a hundred years ago: Percy Bysshe Shelley. Certainly, the social conscience which, human blindness and laziness notwithstanding, is increasingly active among us, and which is evidenced in the work of half a dozen moderns, is the very spring of Shelley's poetry.

But if our attention is concentrated on the shifting present and on the discoverable secrets of nature, not a few of us share the nostalgia for permanence, for ultimate perfection and absolute truth that harassed the so-called "romantics" of the early nineteenth century. And we feel more than a twinge of sympathy when we read words that were written some fifty years ago: "One day, perhaps, we may come to forget the distant horizon, with full knowledge of the situation, to be content with 'what is here and now'; and herein is the essence of the classical feeling. But by us of the pressent moment, certainly, ... Coleridge, with his passion for the absolute, for something fixed where all is moving, his faintness, his broken memory, his intellectual disquiet, may still be ranked among the interpreters of one of the constituent elements of our lives." Substitute for the name Coleridge the name of Conrad Aiken, of Walter de la Mare — and however different the accent, however lacking in Coleridge's Teutonic solemnities, the outlook of these contemporaries, is it not true that they are filled with the same unease, and are trying to charm it to sleep with the same melancholy, hypnotic music that was his portion?

> Sweet will it be lapped round with ease
> And music-troubled air,
> To hear for a moment on the wind
> A sound of far despair...

And then, to close the window fast,
And laugh, and clap soft hands,
While girls from Tal and Mozambique
Parade in sarabands.

Thus Aiken. And now de la Mare:

> Noonday to night the enigma of thine eyes
> Frets with desire their travel-wearied brain,
> Till in the vast dark the ice-cold moon arise
> And pour them peace again;
> And with malign mirage uprears an isle
> Of fountain and palm, and courts of jasmine and rose,
> Whence far decoy of siren throats their souls beguile
> And maddening incense flows.
> Lo, in the milken light, in tissue of gold
> Thine apparition gathers in the air —
> Nay, but the seas are deep, and the round world old,
> And thou art named, Despair.

One cannot match these lines with any specific piece by Coleridge, and yet they seem somehow burdened with a grief not far from that of the man who killed the albatross, and winged with a fantasy somehow similar to that of Kubla Khan's architect.

It is a lonely thing to be without faith, and well might those who fathered this generation of poets cry "Tom's a-cold!" But if the men of the nineteenth century were much scourged by doubts and sometimes stripped by disillusion, they also had moments of sunny confidence that science might yet unravel the riddle of the universe. This is the triumphant prophetic mood of the lyric of Earth in the final act of Shelley's Prometheus Unbound:

BABETTE DEUTSCH

> The lightning is [man's] slave; heaven's utmost deep
> Gives up her stars, and like a flock of sheep
> They pass before his eye, are numbered, and roll on!
> The tempest is his steed, he strides the air;
> And the abyss shouts from her depth laid bare,
> Heaven, hast thou secrets? Man unveils me; I have none.

The query is rhetorical. The secrets of Heaven itself are about to be bared, and Earth rejoices with a kind of dedicated bacchic frenzy in yielding up her own mystery. The seas and the skies alike having been charted, lands and planets remote beyond hazard having been discovered, adventure having salted the tail of the last unicorn, what province remains for man to explore?

What province, indeed, but his own soul? Nature may be clear to him, but not human nature. And with the same excitement, the same hardihood, perhaps, too, something of the same lust for power as the early navigators, the poet takes ship for the difficult, dangerous, extravagantly rich Indies of the human psyche. The Victorian poet who eminently represents this absorption in man, as distinct from that in plumbing the cosmos, is of course Robert Browning. For all his professed belief that God's in His heaven, all's right with the world, he knew enough about men and women to realize that for many people the world has a way of getting out of joint, and it is thanks to Browning's pioneer work in psychological poetry that the modern, who lacks Browning's serene faith, can make the most of his knowledge. It is to this Englishman of the Victorian period that such various twentieth century Americans as Ezra Pound, Edwin Arlington Robinson, Robert Frost, trace, in diverse fashion, their origins. Pound makes oblique acknowledgment in the first of his Three Cantos:

> Hang it all, there can be but the one "Sordello,"
> But say I want to, say I take your whole bag of tricks,
> Let in your quirks and tweaks, and say the thing's an art-form,
> Your "Sordello," and that the "modern world"
> Needs such a rag-bag to stuff all its thought in;
> Say that I dump my catch, shiny and silvery
> As fresh sardines flapping and slipping on the marginal cobbles?
>
> ... And for what it's worth
> I have my background; and you had your background,
> Watched "the soul," Sordello's soul, flare up
> And lap up life, and leap "to th' Empyrean";
> Worked out the form, meditative, semi-dramatic,
> Semi-epic story; and what's left? ...
>
> Such worlds enough we have, have brave décors
> And from these like we guess a soul for man
> And build him full of aery populations ....

The décors that Pound uses considerably differs from the scenery set up by Frost, and his stage sets are rarely employed by Robinson. Yet all three "guess a soul for man and build him full of aery populations," just as all three, though never to be confounded one with another, have tried their hands at the meditative, semi-dramatic form that is proper to the biography of a mind.

Frost, though so notable a master of the dramatic monologue, and so shrewd a chronicler of men and women, is perhaps less close kin to Browning than to another poet of the nineteenth century. His habit of dealing with the daily commonplace, especially the commonplaces of rural life, his interest in giving the values of poetry to speech that can scarcely be unraveled from a loose colloquial prose — what are these but the incarnation of the ideas laid down by Wordsworth in his Preface to the Lyrical Ballads? And indeed, Wordsworth is the fountainhead of much modern poetry, in spite of the fact that his large view of the universe, and of man's place in nature, seems so remote from the post-war mood of bleak agnosticism. It was he, as we have noted, who first enunciated the principle of using the language commonly in men's mouths to describe the events of common life as the basis of noble poetry. And when certain contemporary versemakers, weary of fin de siècle lutes and lilies, finding fantasy withered and glamour stale, followed Synge's injunction to seek "the poetry of ordinary things," they were doing nothing more revolutionary than returning to the Wordsworthian tradition.

If these analogies hold good, it might be asked in what respects, if at all, the poetry of our time differs from that of the preceding century. That it does differ one realizes most clearly by imagining a leaf or two of Ezra Pound or Sandburg, of Yvor Winters or Edith Sitwell bound by mistake into an old-fashioned anthology, Palgrave's Golden Treasury, for example, and considering what a start it would give one to come upon it there. Why should this be so? We have seen that the moderns have substantially the same background as their predecessors and to a large degree the same point of view. The prerequisites for poetry would seem to be an experience passionately grasped, grasped with intensity, and a control of the medium in which it is to find expression. The experience of the moderns does not differ essentially from that of the poets of other days. Women are still fickle and men unfaithful; our little life is still rounded by a sleep, in which we know not what dreams may come; flowers and the sea and the moon are still enchanting; in short, love and death and beauty pierce us no less surely than they pierced men in Shakespeare's day or in Tennyson's. What has altered is not the substance of the poet's experience, but its setting, and its tempo.

The process of attaining mechanical efficiency at the expense of spiritual sufficiency has been tremendously speeded up. That is, in effect, what we mean when we speak of living in a "jazz age." Jazz, if I am not mistaken about a much discussed but still obscure subject, is reducible to syncopation, and the word syncopation, interestingly enough, derives from a Greek word meaning to cut short. In medicine the term is applied to a brief lapse of consciousness or a state of shock. Jazzed music might be described as music that has a moment of faintness and then the emphasis of recovery. And a jazz age is an age when we have to make up for our spiritual lapses by a stressing of material fulfillment, a quickening of all our external activities. This is metaphor, of course, and metaphor is utterly unscientific, but it is also the language of poetry, and may be closer to the truth than bare logic. Life, as Professor Whitehead has observed, used to be passed in a bullock-cart, and in the future it will be lived in an airplane, "and the change of speed amounts to a difference in quality." Certainly, the speeding-up process, the jazz approach, is the very antithesis of the poetic approach, which is in essence not action, but realization.

The improvement in transportation and communication has narrowed the world to such an extent that the depths of the Sargasso Sea have become almost as familiar to us as the surface of a country brook. Darkest Africa is provided with Singer sewing-machines, and every smart drawing-room is presided over by an African negro god. The change in our economic system from a gold basis to a credit basis has meant that we no longer look to India for precious metals but as a market for cotton-goods. All this is destructive to the romantic attitude, if we interpret romance as an attachment to strange, far-off things. We no longer wonder and marvel: we, all too drearily, know. But the effect has not been merely one of disillusionment. It has bred in us a healthy impatience with those who can discern beauty only far away. We are inclined to be a little scornful of the Miniver Cheevys, the helpless tender-minded, who curse the commonplace and eye a khaki suit with loathing, missing "the medieval grace of iron clothing."

Further, the increased intimacy with places remote from us in space and in mental outlook has taught our poets to survey their immediate surroundings with the eyes of a Chinese sage or a Hindu mystic, and to express themselves as nearly as possible with the peculiar terseness of the Japanese lyricists or with the fierce sensuousness and the reliance upon repetition of the Afghan minstrel. That they may improve their technique by thus playing the sedulous ape is fairly certain. But it is less certain if they will at the same time deepen their understanding of their own world. One remembers that Longfellow, a scholar and a gentleman of parts, especially foreign parts, is a mere poetaster beside Emily Dickinson, who scarcely stirred from her own door-step.

Coincident with the changes mentioned above, the development of psychology, whether we embrace the doctrine of the Freudians or that of the behaviorists, and even if we cannot accept either as a complete account of human nature, has rendered us distrustful of our reasoning powers, and at the same time made us rather disrespectful toward our emotions. Nearly seventy years ago Pater was writing: "Modern thought is distinguished from ancient by its cultivation of the 'relative' spirit in place of the 'absolute'." It is not impossible that we are eager to accept the Einstein theory in its vulgar version of "everything's relative" because it premises an instability that we have discovered in our own situation. Where everything makes for confusion worse confounded, what does the poet do?

There is one thing that he does not do: he does not attempt to write a long poem after the fashion of his great predecessors. Milton wrote Paradise Lost in an effort to "justify the ways of God to man." We have given up hope of such a justification. We would be equally hard put to it to justify the ways of man to God. Dante, before him, threw a net of poetry around that entire complex that we call the middle ages. But he was able to do this because he dealt with a stable social order and a solid tradition. We have neither. Wordsworth, after him, was bent on composing "a philosophical Poem, containing views of Man, Nature and Society," thanks to which we have the Prelude and the Excursion. It would be a hardy contemporary who would attempt to set down views concerning Man, Nature and Society, when all three are controversial subjects, and at least two — man and society — seem to be in a state of flux.

The lack of a synthesis such as was provided by the faith of the middle ages and the personal philosophies of a Milton and a Wordsworth center the modern poet's attention upon mere fragments of experience. If he does write a long poem it is apt to be in imitation of Chaucer, who was primarily a story-teller. So we find Masefield, who is often considered the first of the "new" poets, tracing his literary lineage back to the fourteenth century. When the Imagists declare that "concentration is of the very essence of poetry," they are unquestionably right. But when they preface that statement by pronouncing themselves in opposition to "the cosmic poet" as "shirk[ing] the real difficulties of his art," they seem to be making a virtue of necessity. "If to give imaginative value to something is the minimum task of the poet," writes Santayana, "to give imaginative value to all things, and to the system which things compose, is evidently his greatest task." It is the misfortune of these lyricists that they have no cosmos to express, in however concentrated a form.

This fact has not merely the negative result of preventing poets from writing another Divine Comedy or a second Paradise Lost. The absence of a comprehensive content for poetry leads its practitioners to an increased interest in form. Where there is not overmuch or where there is bewilderingly too much to express it is possible — and delightful — to experiment with the manner of expression. So we find that to no small degree it is differences of technique that distinguish modern from old-fashioned verse. And it may be observed in passing that English poets from Chaucer to Robert Bridges have evolved so many beauties in the manipulation of metre that free verse seems to have been the only answer to the demand for a new invention.

As we saw earlier, however, it is words rather than rhythm that are the essential substance of poetry. And it is in their novel use of words that most of the poets mentioned above — Pound, Sandburg, the Sitwells — and others too numerous to mention, prove that they belong to our own day. They reject words that have been worn flat and dull with passing from one hand to another. Sandburg uses new-minted slang. Pound and the Sitwells use old words, perhaps, but stamp them with fresh meanings — meanings that are sometimes unclear to all except the poet's immediate coterie, but that with sympathetic attention, may be understood and enjoyed by outsiders, as, after a sufficient period of hisses and booings, the peculiar idiom of such a musician as Stravinsky or such a painter as Matisse comes to find favor with the multitude.

But words, after all, are symbols for things as well as for ideas, and the greatest danger that the machine age presents to poetry is not that it hurries us along too fast, or shrinks our horizons, or robs us of a comprehensive philosophy, but that it forces us to live in a world of abstraction as empty of emotional values as the algebraic symbol x. Men no longer use tools. They tend machines. And that verb marks an immense change in habits of thought and work. They are no longer familiar with the processes that govern their lives. The fundamentals of getting food and shelter that were the natural concern of the savage and the squatter have become, in our urban and mechanized existence, so complicated that they are now in the ken of a handful of technological experts only. Not the farmer and the artisan but the engineer is now master of the situation — a dangerous state of affairs, as certain far-sighted and tough-minded citizens have recently pointed out. For too many people life has become merely a monotonous pulling of levers and pushing of buttons, between intervals of being shuttled back and forth underground like so much waste matter. This divorce from concrete realities is a distinct menace to poetry, which, oddly enough, cannot soar into the empyrean unless it can also walk the common earth.

The implication is not that machines cannot be touched upon in poetry. Wordsworth once and for all answered the objection to the treatment of seemingly non-poetic themes. "If the labors of Men of science," he wrote, "should ever create any material revolution, direct or indirect, in our condition, and in the impressions which we habitually receive, the Poet will sleep then no more than at present; he will be ready to follow the steps of the Man of science, not only in those general indirect effects, but he will be at his side, carrying sensation into the midst of the objects of the science itself. The remotest discoveries of the Chemist, the Botanist, the Mineralogist, will be as proper objects of the Poet's art as any upon which it can be employed, if the time should ever come when those things shall be familiar to us, and the relations under which they are contemplated by the followers of these respective sciences shall be manifestly and palpably material to us as enjoying and suffering beings."

Let us forget science for a little and consider the industrial revolution which science made possible, and the mechanistic civilization which it produced. The elements of this civilization — machines, engines, dynamos, the whole set of dehumanized devices for providing and distributing the materials of existence — the elements of this civilization are not, essentially, familiar to us. They are not manifestly and palpably material to us as enjoying and suffering beings. They are not familiar to us because they are too complex to be understood except by a very few of us. They are not material to us as enjoying and suffering beings, because we cannot respond emotionally to a machine which we do not comprehend and which we could not possibly construct without the use of other machinery and much highly technical information, as we respond to the homely, humble, intimate tools that we can create after a fashion with our own hands and can certainly control.

For this reason, poetry, when it treats the elements of our civilization, treats them, generally, from a respectful distance. There are poems praising the beautiful precision, the noble organization of machinery. But there are no poems that are able to invest it with the warmth of passion that is bestowed upon a mere mouse, a common daisy, a house that is made with hands and inhabited by enjoying and suffering beings. MacKnight Black's lyrics, which presume to achieve the miracle, make machinery acceptable by speaking of it in human terms.

There are also any number of poems that lament the inhumanity of the present order of things, and more particularly the dehumanizing effect of the factory system. Insofar as machinery has the power to cripple and kill, it affects us emotionally and is the proper subject of poetry. No one will deny that it does cripple and kill, both actually and figuratively speaking. But, on the other hand, crippling and killing is not, except in the case of machine guns, its prime reason for being, and so it enters into our lives and into our poetry in an oblique, indirect, tangential fashion.

Poetry, indeed, though it must be affected by our civilization, is none the less a direct protest against things that are among the chief elements of it. We are living in an industrialized, a mechanized, a standardized world. Now if there is anything that poetry is not, it is not mechanical, and it is not standardized. It is fresh and living, a thing, to paraphrase Shakespeare, that quickens him that gives and him that takes. Poetry, unlike modern plumbing, has no ulterior purpose. It has, indeed, the excellence of a thing that is an end in itself. In an age when most men have their eyes on the main chance, this art is peculiarly important. And we may well be grateful that even in a machine civilization, poetry is still read and written, as virtue is still practiced, for its own sake.

CHAPTER FOUR
WHITHER POETRY?

SPECULATION about the future of poetry is perhaps an idle if entertaining game. But we may see a bit more clearly where we stand by looking not merely back toward our starting-place but forward along our probable road. One of the first questions that arises in any such consideration is whether poetry will remain with us at all. We have seen that our lives are governed by the abstractions of science and rendered dull and empty by a divorce from concrete realities — facts that spell danger to an art which means immersion in experience for its own sake.

All men turn poets when they are in love, and poetry might almost be defined as a falling in love with whatever its subject matter may be: a flower, or a faith, or an idea. It invests it with the emotion of the lover; it sees it, as he sees the beloved, under the aspect of eternity; it seeks the definitive word, the expressive music that will somehow convey its quality. Such treatment is possible in dealing with things like the sky and the sea, though the first is impersonal and the second notoriously inhuman. It is not yet possible in dealing with the machine. Sea and sky have been affecting men's lives and working upon their imaginations and emotions since the days of the psalmist. But the machine is new and constantly changing. One's feeling for the ocean is only slightly modified by the fact that one travels over it in a modern steamer rather than in the galleys of the Greeks. It is the same ocean still. But the telephone and the automobile alter as quickly as man's inventiveness and competitiveness permit. Until the elements of our civilization become as familiar to us as the elements of the non-industrial, non-mechanical civilization were to the artisan and the farmer of a hundred years ago, we cannot incorporate them into the body of our poetry with success. But if poetry must deal with familiar things, it is none the less true that it can endure only through change, and the gradual assimilation of new subject matter is hopeful for the continued practice of the art.

That it is possible, for example, to write poetry about airplanes which is not thoroughly pedestrian, the following lines prove:

CLOUDS

Earth dies to haze below, the cables sing,
The motor drones like some gigantic fly,
A monstrous mound of vapor bathes my wing
And backward with the wind goes sweeping by;
Above the voids white crags go sharp and dim,
Oaks wave, the discs of rootless islands swim,
And arches climb and crumble in the sun
Over gray dinosaur and mastodon.

Earth, dim and fluid, seals the ragged spaces
Where misty islands meet and part below;
Cities that mask eternal hungering faces,
Black wood and water mingle in its flow.

BABETTE DEUTSCH

> Down, down ten mountain heights beneath this floor
> Of marble-smooth and marble-solid air,
> The shout and pride and color are no more
> Than moon-faint mottlings. Distance does not spare.
> They are the clouds now. Icy-lipped I ride
> A window-floor immeasurably wide,
> Firmer than rooted stone. And through its glass
> I watch their formless, sunken shadows pass.

Their author, Frank Ernest Hill, is himself an aviator, and therefore, unlike most of those who versify about it, he knows the actuality of flying. His few lyrics dealing with that experience prove at once that it is possible to write good poems on so novel a subject and that there remain wide fresh fields, in a literal as well as a figurative sense, for the poet to explore. The machine age, while cutting him off from certain experiences, is able to offer him new ones that will become more completely his possession insofar as they become the intimate possession of his fellows. Moreover, the time is still far off when men will refresh their energies with compressed food tablets synthetically composed in a laboratory, when procreation will be effected in a test-tube, when old age will have ceased to torment us, and death be delayed until it is as acceptable as the tokens of maturity have ever been to youth. Until that time comes, the fertile or hostile earth, the uneasy lover, the mother with her child, the pitiful ancient, the unanswering dead, will not cease to stir our blood and trouble our thoughts, and so will remain as they have remained for these thousands of years, the constant matrix of poetry.

But if poetic material changes relatively little, the mode in which it is cast is continually shifting. These changes of technique are to some extent a mere swing of the pendulum: an exhaustive playing with metrical schemes breeds an impatience of them that results in the development of free verse, and when this becomes tedious, the poets flock back in a body to their experiments with meter. But to some degree technique may be affected by purely external circumstance. Before the advent of the printing-press, verse was sung or intoned. When reading was no longer the exclusive privilege of the few, the musical quality of verse altered and, as time went on, suffered neglect. This Chanson Innocente by E. E. Cummings is a fairly typical instance of the way in which he makes typography and punctuation assist in the work that is normally required of meter and verbal texture only:

In Just —
spring when the world is mud-
luscious the little
lame balloonman

whistles   far   and   wee

and eddieandbill come
running from marbles and
piracies and it's
spring

when the world is puddle-wonderful

the queer
old balloonman whistles
far   and   wee
and bettyandisbel come dancing

from hop-scotch and jump-rope and

it's
spring
and
    the
              goat-footed
BalloonMan   whistles
far
and
wee

If poetry recitals should come increasingly into favor in the great urban centers (the rural districts enjoy a vulgar version of them at present), the radio may lead the poets to appeal once more rather to the ear than to the eye, and a more naively musical and perhaps a more largely narrative poetry may come into vogue.

The remote effects of the radio are incalculable. The *Manchester Guardian* ran an editorial recently commenting on the fact that the careful accents of radio announcers are "sapping and must continue to sap the distinctive talk of our fathers, and generations to come, in a Britain delivered over to 'correct' speech, may awaken too late to a realization that they have no means of knowing how much more rich life was in variety when one could make a fair guess at the county, the strath, sometimes even the suburb that a fellow-countryman came from in the course of a few minutes' talk." The editorial writer noted that gramophone records of dialect speech are being made in Yorkshire "to demonstrate to the emasculated Yorkshiremen of the future how sadly they have strayed from the robust and racy speech of the men of old."

In the United States, where, if dialects are less pronounced, distances are greater, New York radio announcers are not so apt to be heard regularly in San Francisco, nor Chicagoans in Louisville, and the distinctive accents of the different sections of the country may not tend to disappear rapidly. This is a good thing for poetry. In the first poem in Josephine Pinckney's memorable little book, Sea-Drinking Cities, the following lines occur:

> The footsteps of the passer-by are hurried
> By these grim women and inimical;
> He calls them witches and resents the fear
> Of arrogant glances that had got him flurried.
> Walking along the water people all
> Speak evil of the trio sewing there.

To the northern ear, lines three and six seem to have an assonantal rhyme, but one fancies that the young Southerner who wrote them heard a perfect chime. Even involuntary assonance has charm, nor is it lessened by one's realization of the effect actually intended.

Certainly, the more local cultures are encouraged, the more diversified language is, the more readily poetry should flourish. It is a vulgar error that this art is something that smells of the lamp. Nothing could be further from the truth. Professor Tucker Brooke says of Shakespeare that he was fortunately not "well-bred and college-trained." Had he been so, he would have been "more precocious and more clever. In all human probability, he would have been very much less wise." And what is true of the greatest poet has a more general application.

Poetry is the flower of the living tongue, and only language that is full of pith and quick with growth can give it color and fragrance. It should not be forgotten that Dante and Chaucer, writing in the Italian and the English of the closing middle ages, were employing language that was the very contrary of bookish. If Dante had held to the academically correct Latin of the time, if Chaucer had chosen the literary French tongue, though both would have been remembered in our orisons, neither, it is very probable, would continue to be read. Of the two dangers that the poet faces, that of being too colloquial and that of being too literary, the second is the worse. If he uses new-minted words that fail to gain permanent currency he will suffer, but if he uses language that is current only among the elect, he will almost certainly die. We have the word of an authority on language, Professor Otto Jespersen, that "poetry is closely related to slang... in so far as both strive to avoid commonplace and everyday expressions. The difference is that where slang looks only for the striking or unexpected expression, and therefore is often merely eccentric or funny... poetry looks higher and craves abiding beauty — beauty in thought as well as beauty in form." That gallows'-bird, Villon, who packed his verse with slang, is still a living figure, whose lyrics we are at pains to elucidate, rejoicing in our rewards, while his correct contemporaries languish in limbo.

Thanks to Mr. Edison, the English we speak will be recorded and preserved, and so will probably be less strange to those who read it five centuries hence than Chaucer's English is to our ears. This is a matter for gratitude, but if the existence of the phonograph and the radio means that pronunciation and diction will become to any degree standardized, the outlook for poetry is correspondingly bad. The changes in pronunciation from Chaucer's time to Milton's, and again from Shakespeare's time to our own, had a definite effect upon prosody. Where Chaucer writes:

"Whan that Aprille with his shoures sote," Milton would have written: "When that April with his showers sweet," losing not only certain syllables but an entire foot, and throwing the meter from iambic to trochaic. Similarly, when Raleigh writes:

> Give me my scallop-shell of quiet,
> My staff of faith to walk upon,
> My scrip of joy, immortal diet,
> My bottle of salvation,

he is able to make his Latin polysyllable longer by a beat than we can. It is noteworthy that Elinor Wylie, who was as close as any writer of this generation to the metaphysical poets of the seventeenth century, delighted to employ the old-fashioned form, as in these lines:

> This web a spider might have spun
> With patience and precision.

Such verbal differences are of first importance to the poet's technique, and the promise of further changes in pronunciation would be a matter for congratulation rather than for condolence as far as he is concerned. One takes refuge in the agreement of philologists that language refuses to stiffen into a mold, but remains fluid and shifting like life itself.

It is not idle to say that the manner of our life will determine the future of our poetry. Genius is no respecter of ages or of persons. It can appear — as the presence of Blake in the eighteenth century testifies — under the most adverse circumstances, and can build its tabernacle in the most unlikely souls. It is as unpredictable as it is unanalyzable. But although the whole history of

English poetry vouchsafes but one Shakespeare, there is a sufficient number of magnificent poets who are not Shakespeares to warrant speculation as to how such others will fare in the years ahead. How they will fare depends in no small part, I think, upon the structure of society.

We have seen that local cultures help rather than hinder the development of art. Fifth-century Athens, which could be set down like another little Italy or little Hungary in the midst of Greater New York and lost there, produced more durable and influential art than imperial Rome. If the American empire follows the Roman model, our poetry must fall upon evil days. If, as many alert observers believe, we may expect within a few decades a series of economic and social wars, we may await no happier result. And if, as a few more sanguine spirits hope, those wars or a less probable bloodless revolution should end in establishing a new order of society, based upon the idea of the world as a group of interdependent states rather than as a group of conflicting empires, we might definitely look for new things.

Where every one had the aristocrat's freedom from worry about necessaries, including the necessity of impressing others with his own importance, the features of an aristocratic society might well become general. Personality would be valued for its own sake, and poetry as the expression of personality would be almost as much a matter of course as an individual style of wearing the hair. This does not imply that poetry would be a slight and delicate thing, exquisite and fragile as the ivories and the lyrics of the Japanese. On the contrary, men would be freer to consider the fundamentals of life than they are in this crowded, confused and chancy world of ours. They would have leisure for thinking about the universe, and about human fate, and being bound neither by the frivolous taboos of the rich nor the fretting harassments of the poor, they would not shrink from thought. Poetry would be fed by philosophy, and would in its turn nourish that vision without which the people perish. Wordsworth's ambition to set down in verse his view of Man, Nature, and Society, would cease to seem impossible of attainment, and might indeed become the task of every serious poet. Alongside the personal lyric that would be almost as common an accomplishment as a good game of tennis is nowadays and as poetry of that sort has always been in a cultivated community, there would flourish the "cosmic" poem that has fallen into neglect.

The rise of major poetry, that is, poetry devoted to issues of more than private significance, may be expected long before any such revolution as will bring in an incredible millennium. Already there are signs that the mood of disillusion and despair, which found its supreme expression in The Waste Land, is beginning to yield to a more mature, if no less sober outlook. The case of man, born into a world which, if not hostile to him, is certainly not cherishing, man — groping toward an equilibrium that he is the first to endanger, being himself the center of unintelligible and conflicting forces, man — spurning the ant that is more purposeful than he, man — measuring the light of distant stars, but in himself mere worm-seed,— the case of man may well be desperate. But if this is true, is it not all the more necessary to find some means of reconciling ourselves to the darkness in which we live and move and have our being, and, if we cannot justify the ways of God, can we not at least justify our own existence by courage and wisdom? The discovery of permanent values is as surely the task of the poet as of the philosopher, and one with which both now appear to be occupied.

In the course of Professor Whitehead's book on Science and the Modern World, a large part of which is given over to a discussion of the poets' views of the universe, he observes that the new knowledge of the physicists is the basis for a new philosophy of nature, one that "must start from an opposite end to that requisite for a materialistic philosophy." Science, he tells us, "is taking on a new aspect which is neither purely physical, nor purely biological. It is becoming the study of organisms. Biology is the study of the larger organisms; whereas physics is the study of the smaller organisms." Certainly an organic as opposed to a mechanistic approach to the universe is attractive to the poet, whom this scientist, for one, credits with being closer to the true nature of things than less visionary men. It is not incredible that philosophy, leaning forward to a less fragmentary and confused view of things, may yet come full circle and meet the vision of a poet three hundred years dead, when he spoke of "the prophetic soul of the wide world dreaming on things to come." This is the proper stuff of poetry, and though we cannot make more of it than Shakespeare did unless we enlarge our own souls, our increased knowledge of the world is one of the first instruments to that end.

At all events, the contemporary poet, as well as the contemporary physicist, is impatient of the materialism that has been governing our thinking for some three centuries. Consider, as a case in point, William Butler Yeats. Yeats has evolved for himself a complicated "system" which is about as full of magic and mystery as a fog at sea is full of noises. But if one strips his work of this difficult and absurd apparatus, one finds at the core of it a preoccupation with the spirit and a desire to declare the bond between the soul of man and anima mundi. Such an attitude is in direct contradiction to the older philosophy of science. True, Yeats does not substitute organism for matter,— he would probably think that too gross a view. But for all his medieval abstractions and quaint superstitions, he has hold, if I understand him rightly, of deep truths: that there is no fundamental quarrel between man and that nature of which he is, after all, a part, and that the growth of the soul is the chief end of man.

In the work of Robinson Jeffers, a poet who is not drawn, like Yeats, into the tangle of theosophical thinking, one finds even more distinctly a vision of the universe large enough to inform a long philosophical poem. It is, in the case of Jeffers, a terrifying vision, but, steadfastly confronted, it has the reconciling gift of all truth. In one of his lyrics he tells us what the substance of a poem must be:

> Permanent things are what is needed in a poem, things temporally
> Of great dimension, things continually renewed in the past and future;
> Fashionable and momentary things we need not see nor speak of.
> Man gleaning food between the solemn presences of land and ocean,
> On shores where better men have shipwrecked, under fog and among flowers,
> Equals the mountains in his past and future.

Permanent things bound together in a cosmic pattern as Jeffers binds them, permanent things edged with the light of our new knowledge of the world, permanent things torn up from the seafloor of emotion and giving off the aromatic odors of fossil resin in the fires of the poet's mind: that is what one is granted in such work as his.

Jeffers' poetry, like that of Yeats, has the supreme value that Whitehead accords to religion. "Religion," writes this philosopher, "is the vision of something which stands beyond, behind, and within, the passing flux of immediate things; something which is real, and yet waiting to be realized; something which is a remote possibility, and yet the greatest of present facts; something that gives meaning to all that passes, and yet eludes apprehension; something whose possession is the final good, and yet is beyond all reach; something which is the ultimate ideal, and the hopeless quest." This passage, which occurs in a chapter purporting to make peace between religion and science, allows us to identify religion with the poetic approach to the world. The work of men like Yeats and Jeffers gives us precisely that: "a vision of something...which is real, and yet waiting to be realized...something that gives meaning to all that passes, and yet eludes apprehension." It is not inconceivable that the poetry of the future should approximate this vision even more closely.

CHAPTER FIVE
CERTAIN POETS OF IMPORTANCE

SINCE, as we have seen, the poetry of our day is necessarily rooted in the past, what seems to be the very latest cry is merely one that has not been heard for several hundred years. Thus, while poets who were considered "new" in 1914 were, some of them unconsciously, following the principles laid down by Wordsworth, those now in revolt against them are using elaborate conceits and mingling a passionate sensuality with an equally passionate concern for the super-sensual, after the fashion of the Elizabethans and the metaphysical poets of the seventeenth century. And it seems not implausible that the youngest generation of poets — those who still have bits of egg-shell clinging to their unfledged wings — will in their maturity fly back to Wordsworth again, not so much for the sake of his technical innovations as for his philosophy of nature. At the same time, it is clear that the process of mechanization going on all about us and the increased tempo of life in this commercial age has given a special slant to modern verse.

Confused and tormented by the undirected forces that dominate our lives, and that showed their potency for evil most clearly during the war, not a few poets try to rid themselves of the nightmare by giving it body and substance in their verse.

BABETTE DEUTSCH

Weary of Victorian sweetness and light, others enjoy outraging the public with a frankness that can scarcely be matched by their seventeenth-century predecessors. And again, there are a number of singers who take refuge in a singularly pure and fantastic music, as remote from the shriek of factory sirens, the iron purr of dynamos, and the clamor of the mob as the faery horns that blow through the lines of Keats and Coleridge.

But while it is possible to assign contemporary poets to one or another of the groups just mentioned, if one examines in detail the work of a particular man, one finds that he escapes classification. The great poets are interesting rather for their special qualities than for that which allies them to their fellows. Nevertheless, by considering a few outstanding individuals, by being attentive to the unique character of their performance, we shall perhaps discover something further about the nature and the trend of modern verse. It seems worth while, then, to speak a little about two or three British and American poets, in the hope that a closer knowledge of the more important of them will help us to understand the poetry of our time.

Curiously enough, the most important contemporary poet England has produced — like her most important playwright and her most influential novelist — is an Irishman. That poet is William Butler Yeats. As a child Yeats lived in Sligo, with his maternal grandfather, the ship-owner, William Pollexfen, a passionate giant whose image little William confused with God and in later years with King Lear. The boy had his grandfather and his mother to thank for the intensity of his nature, but to his father, John Butler Yeats, he owed a more complex debt. It was his father who taught him to feel that, as an artist's son, he "must take some work as the whole end of life and not think as the others [did] of becoming well off and living pleasantly." But unlike his father, who was a follower of John Stuart Mill, the lad needed a faith in which to rest. So when he was seventeen he created a religion of his own, "almost an infallible church of poetic tradition, of a fardel of stories, and of personages and emotions, inseparable from their first expression, passed on from generation to generation by poets and painters with some help from philosophers and theologians." He desired to recreate the folklore of Ireland, to give shape and vitality to the heroically imagined figures whose personalities had grown, he felt, "out of the deepest instinct of man, to be his measure and his norm." And he thought to do this with a vocabulary so sensuous and musical that it would be the natural heritage of Irish poets to come.

There is no question but that he summoned up before his race an image of greatness by the sheer force of his own vision. It is more doubtful whether he has wrought a vocabulary that will be transmitted to later generations of poets. Every writer must make his own style, as every man makes his own memories. Yeats came to realize this, and was indeed not slow to upbraid the beggarly poetasters who aped what they could not create, as is indicated by the lines addressed To A Poet Who Would Have Me Praise Certain Bad Poets, Imitators of His and Mine:

> You say, as I have often given tongue
> In praise of what another's said or sung,
> 'Twere politic to do the like by these;
> But was there ever a dog that praised his fleas?

And with only a shade less of scorn he declares:

> I made my song a coat
> Covered with embroideries

> Out of old mythologies
> From heel to throat;
> But the fools caught it,
> Wore it in the world's eyes
> As though they'd wrought it.
> Song, let them take it
> For there's more enterprise
> In walking naked.

As the foregoing indicates, the poet came to abandon the ornamental richness of his early manner, to write in a loose unrhetorical rhythm and with an almost prose simplicity. It is told of a famous Chinese poet of the eighth century, Po Chu-I, that he was "in the habit of reading his poems to an old peasant woman and altering any expression which she could not understand." And it is the image of an old peasant that Yeats seems to have kept before him in the work of his middle period:

> Although I can see him still
> The freckled man who goes
> To a grey place on a hill
> In grey Connemara clothes
> At dawn to cast his flies,
> It's long since I began
> To call up to the eyes
> This wise and simple man.
> All day I'd looked in the face
> What I had hoped 'twould be
> To write for my own race
> And the reality:

POTABLE GOLD

> The living men that I hate,
> The dead man that I loved,
> The craven man in his seat,
> The insolent unreproved
> And no knave brought to book
> Who has won a drunken cheer,
> The witty man and his joke
> Aimed at the commonest ear,
> The clever man who cries
> The catch-cries of the clown,
> The beating-down of the wise
> And great Art beaten down.
> Maybe a twelvemonth since
> Suddenly I began,
> In scorn of this audience
> Imagining a man,
> And his sun-freckled face,
> And grey Connemara cloth,
> Climbing up to a place
> Where stone is dark under froth,
> And the down turn of his wrist
> When the flies drop in the stream;
> A man who does not exist,
> A man who is but a dream;
> And cried, "Before I am old
> I shall have written him one
> Poem maybe as cold
> And passionate as the dawn."

The cold and passionate quality of his later work is not so readily imitated by other lyricists, although it may eventually put his verse in the mouth of the general, and thus give it a longevity that it would not otherwise enjoy.

It was a sign of health that, robbed of the faith in which he had been nurtured, Yeats should have made his own religion, for awareness of the superhuman is an essential fiber of great poetry. And so, though his religion, no less than that which he rejected, lacks the sanction of the intellect, it is to be valued because it is largely responsible for the splendor of his verse. The same healthy instinct that prompted him to create his own cosmogony saved his work from the taint of mere literature. He understood at the opening of his career that if he wrote sincerely and naturally, not from observation, but out of the deeps of experience, he would, provided his life was an interesting one, "be a great poet." It is this fundamental sincerity, this hatred of whatever is facile, casual, unrealized, joined with his fervent sense of powers now beyond our knowledge, if partially within our control, that gives his work its strength. Nor can one discount the fact, which Yeats has wisely stressed, that his life has been an interesting one. If, instead of traveling up and down Ireland, trafficking with the noblest minds of three generations, standing in the thick of the political fight that has clouded the eyes and choked the throats of Irishmen these several centuries, knowing with equal intimacy the face of poverty and riches, of deep love and arrant hatred, during more than three-score years, Yeats had spent his days digging potatoes in a dingy garden or clerking in a fashionable shop, we should not now have this store of verse from the man. But it was granted him to believe heartily, to feel intensely, and also to live fully, and out of this experience, this emotion and this faith he has wrought enduring poetry.

It is true that his intricate, subtle and incredible "system" is all but beyond the unraveling of shrewd intellects, not to

POTABLE GOLD

mention simple minds. But the greatness of his verse lies in the fact that whether he speaks of love for a woman, pity for a child, scorn of the mob, or the necessity of fashioning his own soul, he speaks in his ordinary voice, without any straining for effect, without rhetoric or undue excitement, out of his personal experience of life. And so, although he deals with unfamiliar legends, and though much of his poetry is informed with esoteric learning, it is saved from unreality, abstraction and thinness by what it sucks up from those knotty roots about his heart. The dictionary defines mysticism as the spiritual apprehension of truths beyond the understanding. Yeats, being a superb poet as well as a mystic, embodies in his verse a sensual apprehension of truths beyond the understanding. His most recently published work, The Tower, shows him a master of the game between spirit and sense which the poet is perpetually committed to play.

It was another Irishman, better known as a dramatist, who, although the body of his verse is exceeding small, gave currency to the theory that governs much contemporary poetry. John Millington Synge, in the preface to his one thin book of lyrics, almost half of which is given over to racy translations, observed: "The poetry of exaltation will be always the highest; but when men lose their poetic feeling for ordinary life, and cannot write poetry of ordinary things, their exalted poetry is likely to lose its strength of exaltation, in the way men cease to build beautiful churches when they have lost happiness in building shops.... Even if we grant that exalted poetry can be kept successful by itself, the strong things of life are needed in poetry also, to show that what is exalted or tender is not made by feeble blood. It may almost be said that before verse can be human again it must learn to be brutal." These words, written in December, 1908, were prophetic. Three years later John Masefield published that narrative poem so abounding in brutality, and so quick with exaltation at its crisis: The Everlasting Mercy. The same month that he finished writing this poem — June, 1911 — he began The Widow in the Bye Street. In the first "story," as he calls these verse narratives, he had, in his own words, "shewn one thing, which often happens in life, the seemingly unworthy man made happy, for no apparent reason," and in the second he sought "to write the opposite, the seemingly worthy woman heartbroken, for no apparent reason." Both "stories" are shot through with the poetry of the commonplace, and where his work is harshest it is most urgent with vitality.

Masefield's craftsmanship is inferior to Yeats', by as much as he is reminiscent of other poets, even the greatest. He is also, in spite of a various and often cruel experience, more tender-minded. But if he ranks a little lower than the angels, he remains a writer to be cherished. His stirring narratives may have been equaled by later comers; they have not, I think, been surpassed. And the finest of those uneven sonnets in which he lifts his praise to Beauty, express the bewildered faith, the desperate hope of more than one generation:

> Flesh, I have knocked at many a dusty door,
> Gone down full many a windy midnight lane,
> Probed in old walls and felt along the floor,
> Pressed in blind hope the lighted window-pane,
> But useless all, though sometimes, when the moon
> Was full in heaven and the sea was full,
> Along my body's alleys came a tune
> Played in the tavern by the Beautiful.
> Then for an instant I have felt at point
> To find and seize her, whosoe'er she be,

> Whether some saint whose glory does not anoint
> Those whom she loves, or but a part of me,
> Or something that the things not understood
> Make for their uses out of flesh and blood.

How much the poetic renaissance which approximately coincided with the war owed to Masefield's performance is hard to say, especially since most of the poets who sprang into the public eye (or shall we say, at the public ear?) in or about 1914 were Americans. It is more probable that the rise of the so-called "new" poetry was a spontaneous growth. But it is astonishing to find how certainly Synge's words were borne out in the work of such different men as Robert Frost, Carl Sandburg, Vachel Lindsay, Edgar Lee Masters, even Conrad Aiken, who was then more under the influence of Masefield than, as he later came to be, that of Laforgue. A "poetic feeling for ordinary life" figures in Frost's genre pictures of New England, in the terse village obituaries by Masters, in many of Edna Millay's sturdy lyrics, and in the cities and wheat-fields of the plain as Sandburg illumines them for us. The work of these Americans, like the Chaucerian narratives of Masefield, the war poetry of Sassoon, the lean sinewy verses of Synge's compatriot, James Stephens, is instinct with "the strong things of life," if it is not always actually brutal. And it is indubitably tender, if it is not often exalted.

I do not forget that there were several poets vocal at that time who were very far from caring about common things and whose work represents the last refinements of technique and sophistication. Among these one may count Ezra Pound, who was attentive to the lessons of Yeats and Browning, albeit he has so individual a voice of his own; Amy Lowell, who performed one tour de force after another, and whose championship of novel poetic methods was of immense help to poets more important if less widely appreciated than herself; H. D., whose hard, clear-cut images are like snow-carvings, frozen into permanence, ivory monuments, marble moments; John Gould Fletcher, with his free-flowing rhythms, his rich abundant metaphor; T. S. Eliot, following Laforgue's dim trail and making a mournful music over the tawdry, the sordid hideousness of modern life.

If I name only Americans it is because the work of almost all of the more notable living English poets belongs to the tradition of nineteenth-century verse. Lyricists like Walter de la Mare, Robert Bridges, Ralph Hodgson, A. E. Housman, — even, though to a lesser degree, Robert Graves, recall the singers of an elder day. It is curious that although this century has produced volumes of superb verse in English, and though many of them were fathered by natives of Great Britain, those poets who have struck a new note have been, with rare exceptions, of American origin. Some of these Americans, like Frost and Pound, were first welcomed in England, and several of them, Pound, again, and H. D. and T. S. Eliot, have spent so many years in the right little, tight little island as to make one half forget that the States may claim them.

But to return to our muttons, or, more precisely, to the very unsheeplike men and women mentioned above as poets who write about extraordinary things and who are innocent of brutality (Pound, be it said parenthetically, is not exempt here, though his violence is of the milder variety that consorts with an ironic temper). It would be possible to speak at length about any one of them, for all of them are rewarding, if sometimes difficult. But let us choose T. S. Eliot, not because he is the most prolific — Amy Lowell was that, nor yet because he is the most fastidious artist — H. D. is that, rather because he has exerted, in spite of the slender quantity of his work and the contumely with which it is not seldom received, so powerful an influence upon his contemporaries.

If one would appreciate Eliot, one must first understand the French poet who exercised as deep a spell over him as he docs over his followers. Jules Laforgue coughed his lungs away at the age of twenty-seven, leaving behind him three thin books, a little sheaf of manuscript, and a small reputation destined to grow incredibly with time. The first gift that Laforgue brought to his verse was a sardonic pessimism, bred by the anchorite years of his early youth, when he was living on two eggs, a glass of water, and five hours of books a day. Accepting Voltaire's diagnosis of solemnity as a disease, he cured it with an irony as deliciously bitter as the kernel of a peach-pit. He enjoyed juxtaposing things vast and grave to the more disagreeable details of human existence, and with a kind of quizzical sentimentality that was essentially unsentimental, he assumed such matters as the moon, winter, telegraph wires, to be subject to the physical and spiritual humiliations that lie in wait for the feeble human organism. Unable to take the anthropomorphic view of the universe which invests man with a false importance, Laforgue reduced man to the least common denominator of the phenomenal world. His verse, like his prose, sparkled with wit and malice. It was thus that he salted his intellectual despair, and kept it fresh.

His temper being what it was, he chose to import into poetry the argot of the street and the jargon of the laboratory. Together with these distinguishing features went a technical skill that showed itself in an artful use of internal rhymes and in the employment of cadence. Laforgue and Gustave Kahn seem to have invented free verse simultaneously in the eighties of the last century, but Kahn sought always a more complex music, while

Laforgue desired rather to convey the immediate sensation with the strictest accuracy possible to an extremely personal idiom. His poetry was more cerebral than sensual, but he opened the gates of the senses to his ideas, realizing that only thus could they fully enjoy the hospitality of the mind.

I have dwelt at such length upon this French poet now nearly fifty years in his grave because in T. S. Eliot, as in Aldous Huxley, Edith Sitwell, some of John Crowe Ransome, much of Conrad Aiken, Archibald Macleish, Hart Crane, Allen Tate, one finds, sometimes clear as the moon at full, sometimes obscured as stars at dawn, but certainly present, the lineaments of Laforgue's temperament. All of these writers share Laforgue's sardonic quality. All of them express a distaste for the world wherein they are condemned to live in verse marked by a style, like Laforgue's, peculiarly personal and often obscure, verse that, like his, deliberately mixes classical allusions with the most sordid commonplaces, thereby sharpening one's vision of the queer hideous puzzle that the universe can present to an analytic mind. Eliot's Waste Land, with its echoes of Webster and the Upanishads, Baudelaire and St. Augustine, its references to Wagner and the latest music-hall ditty, its reliance upon the elaborate researches of Sir James Frazer and other students of dead religions, its moments of startling beauty and equally startling ugliness, above all, its unqualified despair, offers the consummation of this type of poetry, which might be described as symbolical-metaphysical. It is symbolical in so far as it aims to express the poet's emotions in phrases and images so bound up with his own associations as to form a kind of private poetic shorthand. It is metaphysical in its concern for man's fate, its desperate brooding over the riddle of the universe.

The poetry of T. S. Eliot and a good many of his disciples is remarkable as an expression of that disillusion and despair which

POTABLE GOLD

seized all these sad young men when they confronted what the war had made not only of their personal lives, but of Europe and America generally. Their mood is rooted in the horror of death that the Elizabethans felt, and manured by all the dismal waste and ugliness of this industrialized, commercialized century. In large measure their work is a lyrical repetition of the implacable fact which the makers of slang, who are also poets after a fashion, state more simply: you cannot unscramble eggs. The very generation, however, that pulled such a dismal face over post-war emptiness and anarchy is blessed with a poet who sees deeper than the surface wounds of our time, and whose powerful strophes embrace a tragic but unflinching philosophy. This artist is Robinson Jeffers.

Jeffers was nearly forty when the publication of a small volume over the imprint of a New York linotyper brought him into sudden prominence. He had been writing for years, but in almost complete obscurity, and the appearance of these magnificent poems was greeted with salvoes of astonished applause. His work is striped with divers colors: the tawny and saffron and blue burning of the stars; the savage rust of ancient bloodstains on one crawling planet; the bitter green of scorn; the protean fires nesting in that dazzling crystal — imagination.

Whitman is his remote ancestor. He employs a large loose strophe that is related to, if dissimilar from, the rhythms of the elder singer. He is even more acutely aware than Whitman, though planted like him in modern America, of continents and ages far from his own. His is the energy that flows like sap through Leaves of Grass, the peace that broods over the seer of These States. But here is none of the easy sentimentality, the weary cataloguing that ruin so large a part of Whitman's work. Jeffers has, along with virility and vision, a skeptic intelligence, a disciplined technique.

If he recalls Whitman to some degree, his work shows even more obviously the Greek influence. Indeed, the title poem of that early volume, Tamar, is a powerful dramatic narrative modeled, like many of his later poems, on the stern lines of the old Greek tragedies, given a native setting and written in a free verse that has in it the long roll and swing of the elder seas. The contents of this little book were shortly reprinted in a much stouter volume, which contained one of the finest pieces the poet has so far produced, The Tower Beyond Tragedy,— a retelling, in Jeffers' long irregular moving cadence, of Orestes' story. The word "Greek" has come to connote for us an Apollonian approach to life, a sense of measure and order and significance, a dignity under the whips of circumstance, a tolerance which, like Christian charity, suffereth long and is kind. We are apt to forget that Æschylus, Sophocles, Aristophanes, Euripides, came of a Mediterranean people, fierce, hot-blooded folk, who made their gods in their own image, lustful and jealous and keen for vengeance, and whose oldest myths centered about incest and matricide. The poetry of the twentieth-century Californian shows the large serenity of Greek thought at its noblest and deals bravely in living terms with their old terrible importunate themes.

Jeffers remains our contemporary in that he is possessed by the apparently interminable tragedy enacted by the human race. He struggles to wrench his eyes from that spectacle. He leaps into a surge of perverse passions as though to cleanse himself from the scurf bred by stale decencies. He shakes those waters from him and is off again, like a sea-hawk. Even in his less successful poems his power is clear, although he wants a sterner self-discipline, a more reticent expressiveness, if pity is to flower out of horror, and a hard grain of wisdom be left in the clenched fist of desperation.

POTABLE GOLD

Because his reach is enormous, it sometimes exceeds his grasp. Throughout, his work exhibits the large allusiveness, the shining plunges that are possible only to a searching, supple, tough-fibered mentality. And, what is supremely important for us in this age of confusion, he seems to have found a peace as firm as granite and as vital as fire. "I have fancied the ocean and the daylight, the mountain and the forest, putting their spirit in a judgment on our books," wrote Whitman. "I have fancied some disembodied human soul giving its verdict." One thinks of Jeffers' books, and more particularly of certain of the shorter lyrics, like this one:

THE CYCLE

The clapping blackness of the wings of pointed cormo-
    rants, the great indolent planes
Of autumn pelicans nine or a dozen strung shorelong,
But chiefly the gulls, the cloud-calligraphers of windy
    spirals before a storm,
Cruise north and south over the sea-rocks and over
That bluish enormous opal; very lately these alone, these
    and the clouds
And westering lights of heaven, crossed it; but then
A hull with standing canvas crept about Point
    Lobos ... now all day the steamers
Smudge the opal's rim; often a seaplane troubles
The sea-wind with its throbbing heart. These will
    increase, the others diminish; and later
These will diminish; our Pacific have pastured
The Mediterranean torch and passed it west across the
    founts of the morning;

> And the following desolation that feeds on Crete
> Feed here; the clapping blackness of the wings of pointed
>   cormorants, the great sails
> Of autumn pelicans, the gray sea-going gulls
> Alone will streak the enormous opal, the earth have
>   peace like the broad water, our blood's
> Unrest have doubled to Asia and be peopling
> Europe again, or dropping colonies at the morning star;
>   what moody traveler
> Wanders back here, watching the sea-fowl circle
> The old sea-granite and cemented granite with one
>   regard, and greets my ghost,
> One temper with the granite, bulking about here?

What would the man who wrote those lines have to fear from such a judgment?

Here we have, then, vocal in our day and generation, more poets than can be discussed in so brief a survey as this, and, at the very least, four strands of poetic imagination. The first is that of Yeats, who expresses a deep preoccupation with the soul in verse that is either enchantingly sensuous or, by virtue of its simplicity and hardness, the epitome of sinewy strength. The second is that of Synge, and, by the same token, of Masefield and Frost and Sandburg: men who dig about the earthy roots of poetry to bring forth winey fruit. The third is that of Eliot, whose work offers a portrait, in somber colors and sardonic lines, of all that is sick and weary and frustrate in these years of mechanic energy and spiritual enfeeblement. And the fourth is that of Robinson Jeffers, whose fiercely passionate, intensely brooding poems are a voice crying in the wilderness, crying upon the mysticism of Yeats to free itself from the swaddlings of magic, crying to singers like Masefield and Frost to look beyond the precious and immediate present toward the pre-human past and the superhuman future, crying to the wretchedness of Eliot to come and warm itself at primeval unquenchable fires.

With such poets as these to reveal our life to us and help us, even in their blackest moments, to bear that life, can we despair either of the age that has produced them or of the art that will survive it?

THE END

www.ingramcontent.com/pod-product-compliance
Lightning Source LLC
LaVergne TN
LVHW041306080426
835510LV00009B/873